TAKE THESE STEPS and BE HEALED

Franklin Walden

Unless otherwise indicated, all scripture quotations are taken from the Holy Bible, New International Version.

Copyright © 1973, 1978, 1984 International Bible Society. Used by permission of Zondervan Bible Publishers.

TAKE THESE STEPS AND BE HEALED

Franklin Walden
P.O. Box 50
Jennings, FL 32053
Franklinwaldenministries.org

All rights reserved under International Copyright law. This publication may not be reproduced, stored in a retrieval system, or transmitted in whole or in part, in any form or by any means, electronic, mechanical photocopying, recording or otherwise, without prior express written permission of the Publisher.

Printed in the United States

ISBN 0-939241-88-9

This book is dedicated to all those who have exercised their faith for a miracle in their lives.
You are a living witness of the power of God.

"But for you who revere my name, the sun of
righteousness will rise with healing in its wings.
And you will go out and leap
like calves released from the stall."
MALACHI 4:2

CONTENTS

Chapter 1
Healing For Spiritual Deficiency 7

Chapter 2
A Prescription For Peace 13

Chapter 3
But I'm Sick! 23

Chapter 4
The Healing In Forgiveness 29

Chapter 5
The View From Above 41

Chapter 6
His Higher Ways 47

Chapter 7
Conclusion 55

> For God so loved the world that he gave his one and only Son that whoever believes in him shall not perish but have eternal life.
> JOHN 3:16

Chapter 1

HEALING FOR SPIRITUAL DEFICIENCY

Even in this day of advanced science, medicines, and technology, the number of people living with illness and disease is incredible. Billions of dollars are invested into research, searching for illusive cures. Hospitals and politicians wrestle with the overwhelming costs of providing health care. So we emphasize proper nutrition, exercise, vitamin supplements, and regular physical check-ups (and I strongly believe we should maintain this temple) but still, the statistics related to sickness continue to rise at a staggering rate.

However, there is a sickness that has a more far-reaching effect than any disease known to man. It is identified in the Word of God as sin. The roots of sin run deep in the spirit of man and it is imperative we deal with this sin-sickness before we can affect any healing for our physical bodies. Why? The Bible refers to physical, mental, and emotional healing as "the children's bread" (*ref.* MATTHEW 15:21-28) or simply put, a benefit reserved for those who have accepted Jesus as their Savior and Lord. So our initial focus of healing should concentrate on getting ourselves right with God. The Bible identifies the problem and the solution.

> For all have sinned and fall short of the glory of God, and are justified freely by his grace through the redemption that came by Christ Jesus. But God demonstrates his own love for us in this: While we were still sinners, Christ died for us.
> ROMANS 3:23-24, 5:8

We put ourselves in right standing with God by confessing our sin and our need of a Savior. Jesus Christ then advocates our case before God, having become the sacrifice for our redemption at Calvary. That act of love and mercy justifies us before a holy and righteous God and gives us access to a storehouse of provision and protection.

The first step, however, is the one you make. As much as God loves you, He will not force you to accept salvation or any other heavenly gift. Throughout the Word of God we see the conditional promises of heaven poured out in response to an act of faith on the part of each individual. And so it is in the case of healing. It requires you to willingly consent to the plan of God. Then, as we meet the requirement of His Word, it places the obligation of healing on God.

> If you confess with your mouth 'Jesus is Lord' and believe in your heart that God raised him from the dead, you will be saved. For it is with your heart that you believe and are justified, and it is with your mouth that you confess and are saved.
> ROMANS 10:9-10

God's forgiveness cannot take place until we accept His gift of salvation by believing and confessing. Then, God is obliged to receive your petition and bring about the healing in your soul. We have His promise in that regard.

> For everyone who calls on the name of the Lord will be saved.
> ROMANS 10:13

Just as I would do in an altar call, if you've never taken this step of spiritual healing to ask God's forgiveness and receive His salvation, you can do so right now. You see, Jesus Christ was more than just a prominent historical figure. He was God's

Son. He lived a sinless life and took our sins upon Himself for our salvation. He died on a cross for those sins and then rose again, to be our justification, which means it is just as if you'd never committed any wrong. Simply believe what Jesus did...<u>and that He did it for you.</u> Confess to Him the fact that you are a sinner and recognize you are separated from Him. Ask His forgiveness.

God hears your prayer, no matter how simple it is. He will receive your prayer of repentance and accept you as His child. That tugging in your heart is the Holy Spirit, God's agent of regeneration, who is waiting to make that change in your inner being the moment you believe and confess. And once you take the step of accepting Jesus as your Savior, you become a candidate for healing in every area of your life. It was Christ's express purpose to bring us an abundance of God's life and healing.

> I am come that they (read 'you') may have life, and have it to the full.
>
> JOHN 10:10b

So take the first step toward total healing in your life right now. His gift of life is extended for the asking!

> You will keep in perfect peace
> him whose mind is steadfast,
> because he trusts in you.
> ISAIAH 26:3

Chapter 2

A PRESCRIPTION FOR PEACE

Let's look closely at this subject of healing from the book of James. James, the pastor in Jerusalem, has specific instructions to his first-century parishioners.

> Is any one of you in trouble? He should pray. Is anyone happy? Let him sing songs of praise.
> JAMES 5:13

Sometimes people think it's all on the minister's behalf to pray them out of trouble. They want to lay all the responsibility on the pastor or the evangelist. I guess it's so they can have somebody to blame if it doesn't happen. No, let's get it right! When you're in trouble, PRAY!

That's why I think trouble finds us every so often. God wants us to humble ourselves and acknowledge that we need His help. We are incapable of coming up with a better plan for our lives than He has already mapped out for us.

> Trust in the LORD with all your heart and lean not on your own understanding; in all your ways acknowledge him, and he will make your paths straight. Do not be wise in your own eyes; fear the LORD and shun evil. This will bring health to your body and nourishment to your bones.
> PROVERBS 3:5-8

So, if you're facing trouble...pray. Are you walking through "dry places" in your life? Pray! Are you struggling on the job, dealing with a family crisis, having a "bad hair" day? PRAY! Spend time on your knees in conference with your heavenly Father. Humble yourself and turn to Him in your time of frustration. He has your answer! He has your peace! He has the power of intervention to come to your rescue!

> "Because he loves me," says the LORD, "I will rescue him; I will protect him, for he acknowledges my name. He will call upon me, and I will answer him; I will be with him in trouble, I will deliver him and honor him.

> With long life will I satisfy him and show him my salvation."
>
> PSALM 91:14-15

Can you ask someone to pray with you and for you? Of course! But don't think you've met your burden of responsibility to God's Word by giving a request to a faithful prayer-warrior. God will surely bless that individual for praying but your situation may not get any better. You pray when you're in trouble!

Does this mean being sick? Not as identified in the context of James' teaching. Troubles, (or "afflictions" as the King James Version translates it), and sickness are two separate problems and each has it's own remedy according to this scripture.

The second half of *vs.*13 gives us the opposite of "troubles." James instructs us to sing if we are happy. It would seem rather obvious that a person who is happy would be in the mood to rejoice. But again, Pastor James is being specific about these joyous times in your life. He points out the necessity of singing "songs of praise." Just as in our times of trouble, we look to God in the "good times" and honor Him for His blessings. In essence, the scripture declares to us: No matter if your days are filled with "happy or sad", direct your prayers and thanksgiving to the Lord. We find a similar admonition by the Apostle Paul to the church at Philippi.

> Do not be anxious about anything, but in everything, by prayer and petition, with thanksgiving, present your requests to God. And the peace of God which transcends all understanding, will guard your hearts and your minds in Christ Jesus.
>
> PHILIPPIANS 4:6-7

Do you want your Christian life to remain on an even keel? Is stability in your faith through the good and the bad times something you long for? Then recognize God is in control at all times, and your dependence on Him is rewarded with a peace which carries you on heavenly wings over life's bumps and bruises with a song in your heart.

I like what Chuck Swindoll writes in his book "Intimacy With The Almighty."

> I want to affirm the importance of relinquishing everything to Him because He is fully trust-worthy. I am finally learning this; it is no longer something I verbalize from a pulpit or write in a book. I'm finally learning that His sovereign plan is the best plan. That whatever I entrust to Him, He can take care of better than I. That

nothing under His control can ever be out of control.[1]

Have you come to that conclusion in your own personal life? Once you do, it takes the stress and fear out of any of life's circumstances.

> Even in darkness light dawns for the upright, for the gracious and compassionate and righteous man. Surely he will never be shaken; a righteous man will be remembered forever. He will have no fear of bad news; his heart is steadfast, trusting in the LORD. His heart is secure, he will have no fear; in the end he will look in triumph on his foes.
> PSALM 112:4,6-8

The Bible gives us a wonderful illustration of what James is teaching here. We can even speculate that some of this sermon may have come as a result of the real-life experiences faced by the disciples. Do you remember the story of Paul and Silas?

> The crowd joined in the attack against Paul and Silas, and the magistrates ordered them to be stripped and beaten. After they had been severely flogged, they were thrown into prison, and the jailer was commanded to guard them carefully. Upon receiving such orders, he put them in the inner cell and fastened their feet in

> the stocks. About midnight Paul and Silas were praying and singing hymns to God, and the other prisoners were listening. Suddenly there was such a violent earthquake that the foundations of the prison were shaken. At once all the prison doors flew open, and everybody's chains came loose. The jailer woke up, and when he saw the prison doors open, he drew his sword and was about to kill himself because he thought the prisoners had escaped. But Paul shouted, 'Don't harm yourself! We are all here!' The jailer called for lights, rushed in and fell trembling before Paul and Silas. He then brought them out and asked, 'Sirs, what must I do to be saved?'
>
> ACTS 16:22-30

We see the exact principles James talks about, lived out in its most basic form. Here are two disciples who were definitely in trouble. They had good reason to feel dejected. Just look at how their service for God had been received by the city! But they made a conscious choice to act in faith in spite of their terrible state of affairs. They prayed. And as they prayed, Paul and Silas must have been lifted up in spirit and gotten happy because they started to sing! And then it was God's turn...

A sudden earthquake, prison doors opened, chains loosened...all miraculously the result of two remarkable individuals doing what didn't come natural. Paul and Silas responded in a spiritual way rather than what the physical dictated. Now look at the jailor. Imagine his horror as he wakes up and finds all the doors to the cells open. He's living in such a state of mental fear that he doesn't even bother to evaluate the situation. His panic has convinced him all the prisoners have escaped and now his job (and possibly his life) is in jeopardy for his failure to guard these criminals.

His mental anguish is the same as many today who are confronted with an overwhelming crisis. We want to throw in the towel, give up, quit; sometimes even to the point of contemplating suicide. But at that critical moment where this jailor was about to take his own life, he hears a voice that jars him back to reality. It's the voice of reassurance that everything is still under control despite the earthquake and the confusion. It affects the jailor in such a dramatic fashion that he is ready to get some of this peace of mind the disciples demonstrated!

How you respond to adversity is a direct witness to those around you. When people see you being at peace when you should ordinarily be going "out of your mind," the curiosity factor is more than they can bear. "What's your secret?" they ask. And right there it opens the door for you to share Jesus, the Prince of Peace, with them.

What does all this have to do with healing? Scriptural healing isn't just in reference to physical ailments and disease. Today, one of the most needed treatments is mental healing. Doctors are dispensing more anti-depressant drugs to help patients cope with day-to-day living. But it's an "artificial" peace. It's only a temporary relief. Pacifying the symptoms only masks the real area of need.

God's prescription provides a supernatural strength and a calm that insulates your heart and mind from anything the enemy throws at you. There is mental stability in an unstable and tumultuous world for the child of God who will take these two daily "pills" of peace (and then call on Him again in the morning)!

NOTES

[1] Charles R. Swindoll, *Intimacy With The Almighty* (Dallas: Word Publishing, Inc., 1996) 72, 73

Now about spiritual gifts, brothers, I do not want you
to be ignorant. There are different kinds of gifts,
but the same Spirit.
There are different kinds of service, but the same Lord.
There are different kinds of working,
but the same God works all of them in all men.
1 CORINTHIANS 12:1,4-6

Chapter 3

BUT I'M SICK!

> Is any one of you sick? He should call the elders of the church to pray over him and anoint him with oil in the name of the Lord. And the prayer offered in faith will make the sick person well; the Lord will raise him up. If he has sinned, he will be forgiven.
>
> JAMES 5:14-15

After dealing with spiritual and mental wellness, James is now ready to focus his attention on physical healing. And once again, we see God's plan differing dramatically from the procedures outlined in modern medical journals. Where we would normally pick up the phone and call our doctor for an appointment, instead we dial the number to the elders of the church. Specifically, you call. Your spouse may be concerned enough to call, your friends and relatives might ask the pastor to drop by and check on you, but the instruction is given to the individual who is sick. Why? When you get to that point of trusting in what God can do rather than in the practice of medical science, your heart will be ready to receive His healing.

The sick person takes the first step of responsibility. You don't complain because you're sick. You don't feel sorry for yourself or criticize others because they're well and healthy, and you're not. A lot of people do that. But when you are ready to take a step of faith toward your healing, you call for the church elders.

Now, let's look at the elders. What is an elder and what is his responsibility? The title of elder and overseer are used interchangeably in the Bible and there is a rather lengthy list of requirements that qualify an individual to hold that position.

> Now the overseer must be above reproach, the husband of but one wife, temperate, self-controlled, respectable, hospitable, able to teach, not given to drunkenness, not violent but gentle, not quarrelsome, not a lover of money. He must manage his own family well and see that his children obey him with proper respect. (If anyone does not know how to manage his own family, how can he take care of God's church?) He must not be a recent convert, or he may

become conceited and fall under the same judgment as the devil. He must also have a good reputation with outsiders, so that he will not fall into disgrace and into the devil's trap.

1 TIMOTHY 3:2-7

An elder must be blameless, the husband of but one wife, a man whose children believe and are not open to the charge of being wild and disobedient. Since an overseer is entrusted with God's work, he must be blameless - not overbearing, not quick-tempered, not given to drunkenness, not violent, not pursuing dishonest gain. Rather he must be hospitable, one who loves what is good, who is self-controlled, upright, holy and disciplined. He must hold firmly to the trustworthy message as it has been taught, so that he can encourage others by sound doctrine and refute those who oppose it.

TITUS 1:6-9

These are some pretty strict standards by which a person qualifies to hold a position as elder. But the elders are supposed to be the spiritual pillars of the local church. In order for the power of God to be demonstrated in the church, it must operate in the chain of authority God has outlined. As the elders meet these requirements, it allows the gifts of the Spirit to be in operation; including the gifts of healing, discernment, and miracles. If the elders do not have these manifestations in their life, they are not up to par with their requirements and can't have the faith of the Spirit of God. But an elder who is doing his best to live by these qualifications can boldly step forward in faith to do his part on behalf of a sick person who has called. And his part is to anoint that individual "with oil in the name of the Lord. And the prayer offered in faith will make the sick person well."

An elder may anoint you with oil and say, "We are praying God will do something for you, and we hope it's whatever is best, that God's will be done." That may be a prayer but it doesn't sound like a prayer of faith! What is "the prayer of faith?"

It is imperative that the elder praying actually believes God can heal. He must attest to the work of healing Jesus accomplished at Calvary. Not only did Jesus die for our sins, He also suffered for the healing of our sicknesses. The elder must believe healing is still an active part of God's operation in the Church. It was an active dynamic in the early Church and the disciples operated in that kind of faith.

> The apostles performed many miraculous signs and wonders among the people. As a result, people brought the sick into the streets and laid them on beds and mats so that at least Peter's shadow might fall on some of them as he passed

> by. Crowds gathered also from the towns around Jerusalem, bringing their sick and those tormented by evil spirits, and all of them were healed.
>
> ACTS 5:12a,15-16

Some elders may believe this kind of healing power isn't for the church today. They may feel this kind of demonstration died with the apostles. Therefore, they couldn't confidently pray in faith for the Lord to heal the sick and raise them up. But the elder who recognizes Jesus Christ is the same yesterday, today, and forever (*ref.* HEBREWS 13:8), that He bore the stripes for our healing (*ref.* ISAIAH 53:5), and placed His Spirit and power in the Church for the spiritual and physical healing of each member of His body (*ref.* 1 CORINTHIANS 12:1-11,27-31) will trust in the Word of God and take his step of responsibility and pray a prayer that's birthed in faith, in the Spirit, and in the power of God!

Now that the sick person has met their burden of responsibility and the elder has acted in faith on his part of the equation, it is now left up to God to complete His part. His healing comes in direct response to the obedience of the sick and the elder. If you go by the Word of God and do what it says, God is obligated by His Word and bound to confirm it. He is faithful to abide by the promises

He has made when we follow the instructions. You have come too late to tell me God doesn't do what He said He would do. If God didn't do what He promised, He would be a liar. God is not a man that He would lie (*ref.* NUMBERS 23:19; HEBREWS 6:18). He is truth. Jesus Himself declared,

> Whatever you ask for in prayer, believe that you have received it, and it will be yours.
>
> MARK 11:24

Chapter 4

THE HEALING IN FORGIVENESS

God not only works on the physical sickness or disability, but also operates on the inner being to promote a total and complete healing. God always places the emphasis on the inner man before the outer man. You see, you can go to heaven with a sick body, but not with a sin-sick soul. I've known many godly saints who died without ever receiving a healing for their bodies. But it is an absolute necessity for the inner man to be healed of the cancer of sin, so James declared, "if he has sinned, he will be forgiven (*vs*.15c)." I have heard teaching where the belief is that everyone who is sick has committed some sort of sin. That philosophy cannot be backed up by the Word of God. As a matter of fact, Jesus had to deal with this line of thought in the minds of his disciples.

> As he went along, he saw a man blind from birth. His disciples asked him, 'Rabbi, who sinned, this man or his parents, that he was born blind?' 'Neither this man nor his parents sinned,' said Jesus, 'but this happened so that the work of God might be displayed in his life.'
> JOHN 9:1-3

So we can't honestly say that because a person is sick, we need to probe for some hidden sin or wrongdoing. But it can sometimes be the case, as we find in the very next verse of James' teaching. It is probably best understood if we read it like this:

> If he has sinned, he will be forgiven. Therefore confess your sins to each other and pray for each other so that you may be healed.
> JAMES 5:15c-16a

James ties his statement in the last part of vs.15 with a detailed explanation in vs.16. The reason we can make this assumption is because he knits both phrases together with the word "therefore." Or, making it really simple and to the point, the sin or barrier will be forgiven by God as a result of the mutual confession between the parties who feel they have been wronged. And here we find another form of healing. It is the repairing or healing of a

The Healing In Forgiveness

breach of trust, friendship, business partnership, or some other relational obstacle. It involves breaking personal barriers of pride, jealousy, self-pity, and the countless other feeble excuses we have for not forgiving one another. How do we know this is really what James meant?

At the end of the last chapter, we looked briefly at a verse of scripture in the book of Mark. It bears a closer examination now. It's part of an interesting story of Jesus cursing a fig tree while journeying from Bethany to Jerusalem. We pick up the scene as they go back the next day along the same route.

> In the morning, as they went along, they saw the fig tree withered from the roots. Peter remembered and said to Jesus, 'Rabbi, look! The fig tree you cursed has withered!' 'Have faith in God,' Jesus answered. 'I tell you the truth, if anyone says to this mountain, 'Go, throw yourself into the sea,' and does not doubt in his heart but believes that what he says will happen, it will be done for him. Therefore I tell you, whatever you ask for in prayer, believe that you have received it, and it will be yours. And when you stand praying, if you hold anything against anyone, forgive him, so that your Father in heaven may forgive you your sins.'
>
> MARK 11:20-25

We always want to focus on the "pray, believe, and receive" part, don't we? But there are some stipulations to go along with this kind of "mountain-moving" faith. Here again, we find a conjunction ("and") tying both thoughts together into one.

We don't have enough "confessing of faults." But we do have a lot of fault-finding. We don't have many people willing to ask forgiveness and forgive. But we're surrounded by people who hold grudges and have a critical and condemning spirit. No wonder the church is sick. No wonder we seek medical help for our nervous conditions and stomach ailments. Confessing of faults and asking forgiveness not only releases the shackles from our inner man, but also releases the physical stresses we put ourselves through by harboring all this in our heart. Inner turmoil puts pressure on the physical organs of the body. But, knowing your heart is right with the Lord and your fellow man brings peace, comfort, contentment...and healing.

James' teaching links healing with forgiveness. Jesus taught the same thing. One of the main teachings of Jesus while He was on earth was the subject of forgiveness. Why? He WAS and IS forgiveness!

When you see Him you see a Deliverer and Healer. When you see Him, you see One who destroys the yoke, who holds the keys of hell and

The Healing In Forgiveness

death, who is the same yesterday, today, and forever! But Peter decided to question Jesus about forgiving.

> Then Peter came to Jesus and asked, 'Lord, how many times shall I forgive my brother when he sins against me? Up to seven times?' Jesus answered, 'I tell you, not seven times, but seventy-seven times.'
>
> MATTHEW 18:21-22

Jesus followed up His response to Peter with one of the most intense parables illustrating the magnitude of healing through forgiveness. It's the story of a king who wanted to settle accounts with his servants. One was found who owed roughly two and a half million dollars. He wasn't able to pay his debt so the order was given that he, his wife, and children were to be sold into slavery and all their possessions liquidated to make the payment. With no other recourse, the servant fell on his knees and pleaded with the king for mercy. He begged for an extension on his debts. The king was obviously touched with this man's petition. Not only was the family spared the tragedy of separation and slavery, but the entire amount owed was cancelled! The king wiped this man's account clean! He didn't ask the servant to get in better financial shape and then make payments. He just completely forgave the debt! It's a fantastic story of mercy, to this point. But it's about to take a tragic turn...

This same servant leaves the court, just having his life and family saved by the mercy of a king. Quite possibly on his way home, he runs into one of his fellow servants. And it so happens to be someone who owes him some money. It's an insignificant amount, a mere fifteen dollars. Imagine the astonishment of the onlookers, as this first servant grabs his fellow servant by the throat and chokes him, screaming, "Pay back what you owe me!" The fellow servant begs him to have a little patience until he can pay him back, but his pleas fall on deaf ears. Instead, the servant placed an injunction against his debtor and had him thrown in prison.

But, some of those who had been in the court with the king earlier that day were in this group of onlookers. It caused them such distress that they went back to the king to report what they had witnessed. And we catch a glimpse of what happened next.

> Then the master called the servant in. 'You wicked servant,' he said, 'I cancelled all that debt of yours because you begged me to. Shouldn't you have had mercy on your fellow servant just as I had on you?'

The Healing In Forgiveness

> In anger his master turned him over to the jailers to be tortured, until he should pay back all he owed.
>
> MATTHEW 18:32-34

Though this servant had asked for mercy originally, he didn't accept the forgiveness of the king. He was glad that his slate had been wiped clean, but he did not receive or apply the spirit of mercy. And then we hear this ominous statement from the lips of Jesus...

> 'This is how my heavenly Father will treat each of you unless you forgive your brother from your heart.'
>
> MATTHEW 18:35

I love to talk about the mercy and love of God. He is a good God. But He is also a righteous and just Lord. And the powerful truth of His justice is that He balances the scales of right and wrong. Often it appears to us that the unjust are living on a greater scale of blessing, prosperity, and happiness than the children of God. But God is faithful to reward each individual according to their way.

> Do not fret because of evil men or be envious of those who do wrong; for like the grass they will soon wither, like green plants they will soon die

> away. Be still before the LORD and wait patiently for him; do not fret when men succeed in their ways, when they carry out their wicked schemes. Refrain from anger and turn from wrath; do not fret - it leads only to evil. For evil men will be cut off, but those who hope in the LORD will inherit the land. A little while, and the wicked will be no more; though you look for them, they will not be found. But the meek will inherit the land and enjoy great peace. The wicked plot against the righteous and gnash their teeth at them; but the LORD laughs at the wicked, for he knows their day is coming.
>
> PSALM 37:1-2,7-13

James was well aware of Jesus' parable as well as the writings of King David. And he incorporated all this into his teaching to the congregation in Jerusalem. He knew something like a spirit of unforgiveness could keep people from being healed spiritually and physically.

> Speak and act as those who are going to be judged by the law that gives freedom, because judgment without mercy will be shown to anyone who has not been merciful. Mercy triumphs over judgment.
>
> JAMES 2:12-13

The Healing In Forgiveness

Now we're ready to discover the powerful impact that forgiveness has on our healing.

> The prayer of a righteous man is powerful and effective.
>
> JAMES 5:16b

The implication of this phrase is that you have taken the necessary steps to forgive and be forgiven. It is then that your prayer becomes powerful and effective because now you are in right standing with God and your fellow man. It is a place where God can freely channel his flow of healing because there is no hindrance or obstruction to you receiving it. This is consistent with what Jesus taught in His Sermon on the Mount.

> Therefore, if you are offering your gift at the altar and there remember that your brother has something against you, leave your gift there in front of the altar. First go and be reconciled to your brother; then come and offer your gift.
>
> MATTHEW 5:23-24

God cannot honor that petition for blessing or healing until reconciliation takes place. Outside of this approach, you will never get what you ask of God. We come to receive from God on the basis of His Word or we leave empty-handed. You can be boastful about how much you love and serve God, you can speak in tongues, you can be baptized and be a long-time member of your church, and bestow your money and effort into furthering the kingdom of God, but your prayers for healing are not recognized until these steps of forgiveness are taken. You may even be a pastor, evangelist, or hold a place of authority in the church, but God doesn't look at what position you occupy. He is looking for a contrite heart that is willing to acknowledge His Word as being the blueprint for our total well-being.

> Forgive us our sins,
> for we also forgive everyone who sins against us.
> And lead us not into temptation.
> LUKE 11:4